The Spirit of

Auvergne

Catherine Pinchetti

PACKARD PUBLISHING LIMITED

CHICHESTER

Dedication

To my students of French

To my mother

The Spirit of
AUVERGNE

© Catherine Pinchetti

First published in 2015 by Packard Publishing Limited, 14 Guilden Road, Chichester, West Sussex, PO19 7LA, UK.

ISBN 978 1 85341 152 6

Cover photos clockwise from top left: Examining herbs at a Fête du Roi de L'Oiseau, Le Puy-en-Velay (Haute-Loire) – photo: Gérard Cavaillès; the statue of Vercingétorix, Clermont-Ferrand (Puy-de-Dôme) – photo: Danyel Massacrier; the dormant volcano, Puy Mary, and Salers countryside (Cantal) – photo: Jean-Louis Faure; the Fortress at Bourbon-L'Archambault (Allier) – photo: Daniel Blanchard; Le Puy lace – photo: Catherine Pinchetti; characteristic Salers cattle – photo: Jean-Louis Faure; Fourme d'Ambert cheese – photo: Ludovic Combe, SIFAM; head of the statue of St James, Le Puy Cathedral – photo: Catherine Pinchetti.

Title page photo of a stoat *(hermine)* by Alain Durand.

Every effort has been made to attribute illustrations correctly, and to obtain permission to reproduce copyrightable images, quotations and extracts appearing in the text.

Edited and prepared for press by Michael Packard

Design and layout by Hilite Design & Reprographics Ltd, Marchwood, Southampton, Hampshire, UK.

Printed in the United Kingdom by PublishPoint, KnowledgePoint Ltd, Winnersh, Reading, Berkshire.

Contents

Introduction

Auvergne conjures up many images.

There are the unspoilt wide-open spaces where one can feel closest to the beginning of time, gazing in wonder at strange and majestic landscapes shaped by the largest concentration of dormant volcanoes in mainland Europe. Their lava stone gave its singular dark hue to much of the local architectural heritage. Auvergne is an outdoor paradise, soothing, invigorating, where air and water retain an eternal freshness, where snow heralds the season of Nordic skiing and dog sleds and where being close to nature is as effortless as breathing. Its purity is reflected in a bottle of Volvic mineral water, whose label featuring green volcanic peaks and craters is familiar to shoppers worldwide. Auvergne was bestowed a treasure of mineral and thermal springs known for their healing virtues for over 2000 years: the spas of Bourbon-L'Archambault, Vichy or Mont-Dore come to mind. This is the heartland of the ancient *Massif Central* in the middle of France. It is within the Occitan linguistic domain and is also an historic Celtic territory. The powerful Arverni Gallic tribe gave its name to Auvergne and supplied a French national legend in the person of Vercingétorix, the gallant warrior who, for a while, made the Roman Julius Caesar doubt his invincibility. This is also the cradle of the Bourbon dynasty of French kings and their European offspring.

There are more images. The region is believed to be representative of mythical 'deep France', where time stands still in a fantasized past. Here you will find provincial towns such as Murat or Monistrol-sur-Loire quietly tucked away, picture-book medieval villages like Blesle, Charroux or Laroquebrou, small churches with precious reliquaries, abbeys or cathedrals full of pilgrims' memories like Orcival or Le Puy, castles with turrets emerging from forests or perched on the rocky islet of a crater lake. You may be drawn to a shop window displaying the provender of the day in ancestral fashion: a basket of mushrooms, bottles of brightly coloured aperitifs made from mountain herbs, a hessian bag of Puy lentils, garlands of dry-cured sausages, slabs of some of the five great regional cheeses. You will be thinking of buying a knife handcrafted by a Thiers cutler or a piece of exquisite Puy lace 'before it vanishes'. If you are even keener to immerse yourself in lovingly preserved rural traditions, follow the *Route des Fromages d'Auvergne* (Auvergne Cheeses Route) or the *Route des Châteaux d'Auvergne* (Auvergne Castles Route), or experience events like the *Fête de la Saint-Cochon* (The festival of Everything is Good in Pigs) in Besse and the Billom Garlic Fair.

This book will not give you an exhaustive list of highlights: choices were made so that you can decide on the path to follow. The selections were made by my students of French, of various ages, backgrounds and nationalities, who demanded more than the acquisition of the language and the conventional touristy background information. They wanted to gain insights into real-life French people, in their own words. In this book, *Auvergnats* from the past or the present speak about their land, through a selection of original French extracts offered with their English translation.

Auvergnats indeed have a strong identity, already noticed by Caesar himself. Isolated by their complex topographical relief and harsh climate for centuries, they were forced to rely on themselves, the solidity of their families and the solidarity of their fellow men. Poverty taught them to make the most of bare essentials, which in turn bred resourcefulness. These children of a demanding and austere land were long considered ignorant and miserly but, undaunted, many of them shared the adventure of migrating to Paris and doggedly worked their way to prosperity. People of substance, courage and intelligence, *Auvergnats* gave France three Presidents of the Republic, the philosopher and mathematician Blaise Pascal, the soldier and statesman Marquis de La Fayette and the *Résistante* Germaine Tillion.

Among the heroes one must not forget to mention Bibendum, the plump Michelin Man made of tyres, and all the maps he promoted! Rural Auvergne, the idyllic land of cattle – specifically bred and hardy beauties enjoying 'France's largest prairie' – is also seriously industrial, boasting the Michelin rubber empire, the Limagrain seeds and cereals giant, biotechnology and cosmetics in Vichy, plastics in Yssingeaux, as well as feeding the French with premium dairy products and meat.

This is the real Auvergne. Nearly half of its 1.36 million inhabitants live in and around the Michelin capital of Clermont-Ferrand – *le Grand Clermont* (Greater Clermont) – but not all of those who have their residence in villages are farmers. They all benefit from the very best high-speed internet cover in the country. ASM Clermont is among the greatest French rugby clubs. The region which was once emptied by emigration now attracts newcomers with jobs, a warm welcome – locals are actually generous – and a promise of a high quality of life. Very small artisan companies coexist with research clusters. Clermont-Ferrand, built with black lava stone and formerly considered 'gloomy', now bursts with the energy of its university students and its Short Film or Jazz Festivals. Le Puy's unusual sloping streets, also black, still gather the crowds of pilgrims bound for Santiago de Compostela but come alive with the colours of Renaissance pageantry during its *Fêtes du Roi de l'Oiseau*. Rural roots foster eco-friendly tourism, the most developed among landlocked areas in France. The French motorway network, which had once avoided this part of the country, is finally well connected to its major cities. Auvergne used to feel relegated to the status of a rural backwater but is now forging stronger ties with dynamic Rhône-Alpes next door, especially with Saint-Etienne and Lyon.

'Auvergne Nouveau Monde' ('A New World in Auvergne') is the new slogan of the region, an invitation to the challenging adventure of drawing upon the images and values of the past to build a harmonious, greener and rewarding future open to all who seek a more wholesome life.

Catherine Pinchetti

Acknowledgements

This book would not exist were it not for my students of French: their enthusiasm and unflagging curiosity were my inspiration. My thanks go first to my editor, Michael Packard, for his patience and support, and for putting the book on the right track. I have then to thank my husband, Don, who was always ready to test-read and offer comments; my daughters Sophie, for preliminary editing when needed, and Juliette for her encouragement. My thanks too go to my friend, Patrick Gauthier, for his valuable suggestions; also to all the committed Auvergne *mairies, offices de tourisme*, associations, companies and individuals for their support over the telephone — their names are listed at the end of the book.

CP

The Moulin de Chambeuil (Cantal) in summer. Photo: Alain Durand.

L'AUVERGNE

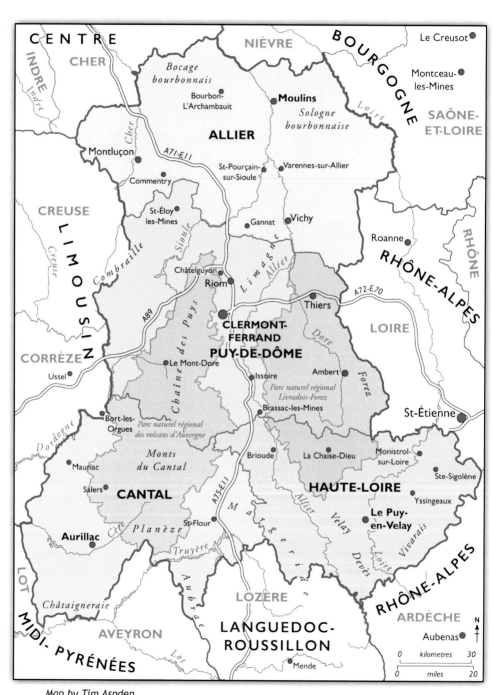

Map by Tim Aspden

Of volcanoes and wide-open spaces

Auvergne used to be considered as the geographical centre of France, which has been calculated to lie exactly in the village of **Nassigny** (Allier). That is true for metropolitan France (including Corsica) but Vesdun (Cher), in the Centre region, claims to be the one for mainland France! However, Auvergne unquestionably is the heartland of the ancient mountain area of the **Massif Central**. It is a world apart, where it is still possible to feel surrounded by the silence and sweeping panoramas of primordial time, and where one can travel for miles without seeing any sign of civilization. A remarkable concentration of dormant volcanoes — first identified in the eighteenth century and estimated to be between 95 000 and 7000 years old — shaped the landscape, leaving a strange and majestic terrain, and thermal springs which are famous worldwide. Unique in Europe, Auvergne displays all the volcanic landforms, from huge domes and cones to calderas and maars (crater lakes), lava pyramids and plateaux, faults, cliffs, or solitary spikes of igneous black rock.

A crater lake in the Cézallier area (Cantal): Photo: Joël Le Pelletier.

How the Auvergne crater lakes came to be

This is the legend of *le lac Pavin*, one of the youngest *Auvergnat* volcanoes in Puy-de-Dôme, whose name means 'Horror'.

Dieu créa l'Enfer pour précipiter Lucifer dedans. Après des années de supplication, il l'autorisa à faire des trous dans l'écorce terrestre afin de pouvoir observer le ciel. Mais Lucifer perça la terre de part en part en formant des volcans. Dieu, très en colère, recouvrit la Terre de glace pour calmer ce brasier et reboucher les trous creusés par Lucifer. Vaincu, Lucifer retourna sous terre et pleura de colère. Comme il craignait que ses larmes n'éteignent le brasier de l'Enfer, il fit en sorte qu'elles s'échappent par les fissures d'un volcan. C'est ainsi que le lac Pavin fut rempli des larmes de Lucifer. [1]

God created Hell in order to throw Lucifer into it. After years of supplications, he gave him permission to make holes in the Earth's crust so he could gaze at the sky. But Lucifer disobeyed and pierced the earth through and through, forming volcanoes. God became very angry and covered the Earth with ice to quench that inferno and to plug the holes hollowed out by Lucifer. Defeated, Lucifer slunk back underground and sobbed with anger. However, fearing that his tears might put out the fire of Hell, he made them escape through the cracks of a volcano. In that fashion, Lake Pavin was filled with Lucifer's tears.

Volcanoes are called *puys* (derived from the Latin *podium*, a mound), *plombs* (an alteration of Occitan *pom*, a rounded summit) or *sucs* (sugarloaf-shaped mountains or craterless volcanoes). Just south of **Clermont-Ferrand**, along a north-west to south-west axis, the **Chaîne des Puys (Monts Dôme)**, backed by the **Limagne** fault and the **Chaîne de la Sioule**, extends over 40 km and numbers 80 volcanoes (**Puy de Dôme**, 1465 m); the **Monts Dore (Massif du Sancy)** have the highest peak in Auvergne (**Puy de Sancy**, 1886m). The **Monts du Cantal** range stretches over 240 km and features the largest cone-shaped stratovolcano in Europe, 60 km in diameter (**Plomb du Cantal**, 1855 m), while the **Cézallier** basaltic high plateau has an outlandish, mysterious beauty. They are all part of the largest European Nature Park, *le Parc naturel régional des Volcans d'Auvergne*, created in 1977: 120 km long and home

The 'Auvergne Virgin', a 50-cm statuette seen here in a niche in a wall in the village of Billy (Allier), carved in typically dark Volvic stone. Photo: Catherine Pinchetti.

to over 90 000 inhabitants, it is an open book on the long and complex historical geology of Auvergne, which generated vastly diverse areas and a distinctive human history. On the eastern side of the region, in Haute-Loire, lies another basaltic plateau, *Devès*, along with the *Velay* and *Forez* volcanoes. The lava stone quarried for centuries in **Volvic** (Puy-de-Dôme) and known as *pierre de Volvic*, with remarkable qualities and hues ranging from black to grey, gives their singular dark appearance to many *Auvergnat* buildings.

The volcanic, basaltic stone used as building material throughout the region, seen here near Murat (Cantal). Photo: Christian Lavollée.

Rent a donkey!

Auvergne can be explored on foot, or by donkey,[2] following the example of the Scottish writer, Robert Louis Stevenson, who in 1878 jolted his way from **Le Puy-en-Velay** to **Saint-Jean-du-Gard** in Languedoc, on the back of his faithful and hardy female donkey, Modestine. He recorded the journey in his book, *Travels with a Donkey*.

In Stevenson's footsteps along an Haute-Loire road. Photo: Catherine Pinchetti.

L'Auvergne, the enduring power of images

Attitudes towards the region

Victim of its largely difficult terrain and harsh climate, consistently depressed economically and under-populated, Auvergne was deliberately bypassed by main roads for a very long time: it was skirted, not penetrated. It was barred from outside influences, and so retained traditions which had been abandoned elsewhere. It is still the kind of place where, in season, wild mushrooms picked only a few hours before are sold in bulk, and by word of mouth, in a local's barn, between a lathe and drying sausages. It is one of France's Celtic areas where the famous and vigorous folk dance, **bourrée**, was born and where

5566. - Une Bourrée à deux

A posed photograph of two Auvergnats dancing a 'bourrée' to music played on accordion and bagpipes ('cabrettes') from an old postcard. Photographer unknown.

people still play the old *Auvergnat* tunes on bagpipes. They also spoke Occitan dialects until the early twentieth century, with the exception of Allier and the northern tip of Puy-de-Dôme.

Paradoxically, the unlocking of Auvergne by the railways in the second half of the nineteenth century only contributed to the mass exodus of *Auvergnat* peasants to the capital. A number of them had previously sought a better life in southern French cities and Spain. In Paris, they would originally scratch a living by selling coal and wine — hence their nickname **bougnats**, a deformation of *charbonniers* or coal-sellers, pronounced with an Occitan accent — until their hard work and tenacity made them prosperous.

Parisian Auvergnats: the value of work and solidarity

Auvergnats started their emigration to Paris around 1880, thanks to the Clermont-Ferrand—Gare d'Austerlitz, Paris train service. Their *bougnat* trade was usually combined with the management and, later, acquisition of a *bar-tabac* or a bistro, or perhaps a hotel.

> *L'arrivée dans la capitale est plutôt effrayante pour qui n'a jusqu'alors connu que son village et ne sait que traire les vaches ... Les gars et les filles qui débarquent parlent à peine français. Est-ce l'une des raisons qui pousse les Auvergnats à se regrouper, les premiers arrivés aidant les nouveaux venus ? ... Chaque village a son amicale, peuplée de visages familiers ... on parle le patois ... On travaille dur chaque jour de la semaine ... Pas le temps pour s'occuper d'un enfant. Alors on envoie le petit dans la ferme familiale, chez les grands-parents ... On embauche des Auvergnats ... On est très tôt plongé dans les groupes folkloriques: ... La Bourrée de Paris est une véritable agence matrimoniale.* [3]

The arrival in the capital is rather daunting for someone who has never gone beyond his village and whose only skill is to milk cows ... The lads and lasses who come off the train can barely speak French. Is it one of the reasons why the *Auvergnats* stick together, those who arrived first giving a helping hand to the newcomers? ... Every village has its support association, whose members are familiar faces ... everyone speaks the dialect ... All work hard, not a single day off ... No time to look after children. The little ones are sent to the family farm, at the grand-parents' ... Jobs are given to other *Auvergnats* ... The young people join folkloric groups early on: *Bourrée de Paris* is like a matrimonial agency.

Still, the highlight of the year for the Parisian *Auvergnat* community today is the folk-music ball called **'*La Nuit Arverne*'** ('*Auvergnat* Night'). Everyone dances to the rhythm of the traditional **cabrettes** (*Auvergnat* bagpipes made of goat skin) which, mixed with the Italian immigrants' accordions, brought about Paris' emblematic **bals musette** in the early twentieth century.

Wood, coal and wine: Bougnats in Paris in the late nineteenth century. Photographer unknown.

A 'bal musette' in Paris, 1931. Photo from Ernest Flammarion's book on Paris of that date. A scholarly account of the origins of Bals Musette and the Auvergnats in Paris is by Marianne Bröcker, 'A French Minority', in U. Hemetek, G. Lechleitner, I. Naroditskaya & A. Czekanowska, eds, (2004) **Manifold Identities: Studies on Music & Minorities**, Cambridge Scholars Press, Amersham, for International Council for Traditional Music (ICTM).

Die-hard prejudices against Auvergnats

Auvergnats and their region traditionally had a negative image, as reflected in an old saying: *'D'Auvergne ne viennent ni bonnes gens, ni bons vents'* ('From Auvergne only bad people and bad winds come'). The people, who had the deplorable habit of pronouncing 's' as 'ch' (*chauchiche chèche* instead of *saucisse sèche*, dry-cured sausage), were supposed to be ill-mannered, backward and penny-pinching, their land only fit for producing cheese. But **Jean Anglade**, born in 1915 and one of the most famous *Auvergnat* contemporary authors — pp. 70-72 — wrote this:

C'est bien connu, l'Auvergnat passe ses journées à compter ses sous, il met ensuite son portefeuille sous son traversin et arrête sa montre en se couchant pour en économiser le ressort ! ... Moi, je ne connais rien de plus beau que le mot de La Fayette – un beau raccourci des qualités auvergnates – qui, lors d'une famine, alors que son intendant lui disait: 'Les cours augmentent, c'est le moment de vendre nos réserves de blé,' lui répondit : 'Non, c'est le moment de donner ! [4]

Everybody knows that the *Auvergnat* spends his days counting his money, then he tucks his wallet under his bolster and stops his watch before going to bed in order to save its spring! ... As for me, I think there is nothing more noble than the word of La Fayette – a concentration of *Auvergnat* qualities – who, during a famine, when his steward was urging him, saying: 'The prices are going up, it is the time to sell our wheat reserves,' answered: 'No, it is the time to give them away.'

Stereotypes of Auvergne still persist: a somewhat archaic land of rugged, tight-fisted farmers, with lots of cows and cheeses, shrinking villages and quaint pockets of old-fashioned crafts – tanning, paper-making, cutlery, lace-making – not to mention the bitter cold and paralysing snow in winter or the stifling heat in summer. It is true to say that 42 per cent of the inhabitants still live in rural areas and that the current increase in population – ending a long period when it kept falling – has to contend with its steady ageing. Almost a quarter of the 1 356 000 *Auvergnats* (2013 figures) are over 60. The region may now be crossed by two motorways, but access to its inner roads remains a challenge in winter. Despite these caveats, Auvergne cattle and cheeses enjoy a high reputation –***Sommet de l'Elevage*** in Clermont-Ferrand is the third largest show for livestock breeders in the world. Environmental awareness now makes the unspoiled spaces of Auvergne attractive to outdoor enthusiasts and appealing to frustrated city dwellers in search of a 'green' quality of life and spacious, affordable housing.

Joseph Canteloube. Bing photos.

Songs of Auvergne

The composer and musicologist **Joseph Canteloube** (1879-1957), whose father was a native *Auvergnat*, spent much of his life roaming the region's countryside to collect its folk songs, which he arranged as the beautiful *'Chants d'Auvergne'* ('Songs of the Auvergne'), published between 1924 and 1955. They are often broadcast over the radio, and played today by local groups promoting *Auvergnat* Occitan. The *Institut d'Etudes Occitanes de la région Auvergne* (IEO) in Clermont-Ferrand is dedicated to reviving the interest in that linguistic heritage.

Georges Brassens, the popular Languedocian singer born in Sète (Hérault) with his characteristic pipe and cat (always called just 'le chat'). Photo: Babelio.

In his song *'L'Auvergnat'*, the popular singer **Georges Brassens** (1921-1981) had paid tribute to the generosity of a native *Auvergnat*. Furthermore, despite its reputation for penny-pinching, Auvergne is one of the French regions whose people give most to charities!

Auvèrnha, an Occitan land

An *Auvergnat* riddle: [5]

'Quat' qui batten lou tzemi	*'Quatre qui battent le chemin*	[What has] 'Four which beat upon the path
Quat' qu'apportent lou sparti	*Quatre qui apportent le déjeuner*	*Four which* bring lunch
Et quat'qu'agaytent li chat.'	*Et quatre qui regardent le ciel.'*	And four which are pointing at the sky.'

[Answer: the cow, which has four hooves, four udders, two ears and two horns!]

L'Auvergne, land of cows

Avec ses 30 000 vaches réparties dans le Cantal, la race aubrac (race de vache auvergnate comme la salers) affiche une progression constante ... L'aubrac est facile à élever ... Elle s'adapte parfaitement aux territoires de la Haute Auvergne grâce à sa robustesse ... Elle assure une bonne rentabilité économique ... Les vaches sont engraissées uniquement à l'herbe. L'herbe, c'est la matière première qui coûte le moins cher. Et pas besoin de transport, donc un bilan carbone excellent. [6]

With its 30,000 cows throughout Cantal, the Aubrac breed [native to Auvergne like the Salers cow] is in constant improvement ... The Aubrac cow is easy to raise ... It is perfectly adapted to the Auvergne highlands, thanks to its robust constitution ... It is remarkably cost efficient ... Cows feed on grass exclusively. Grass is the cheapest diet. No need for transportation either, so its carbon footprint is enviable.

A poster promoting AOP Auvergne cheeses; (left to right) Cantal, Saint-Nectaire, Fourme d'Ambert, Bleu d'Auvergne and Salers. Photo: Association des Fromages AOP d'Auvergne.

The great Auvergne cheese tray

The above cheeses are the great *AOP* (PDO Protected Denomination of Origin) Auvergne cheeses. The scenic **Route des Fromages d'Auvergne** will delight your eyes and tastebuds. For a very long time, *Cantal* cheese was as good as money for trade between Languedoc wine-producing areas and the Auvergne highlands.[7]

A Buron in the Auvergne countryside. The roof slopes down very low, giving the buildings their characteristic A-shape. Photo: Joël Le Pelletier

Auvergne cheeses in general used to be made in '*burons*' — 'cheese cabins', built of dark basaltic lava stone with characteristic stone shingles or '*lauzes*' — from mid-May to mid-October. The buildings were deserted in the mid-twentieth century because of the hardship of the *buronniers*' life and the modernization of production. The few still standing have been turned into rustic restaurants and *gîtes*, or preserved for cultural reasons, mostly in Cantal. Today, Auvergne accounts for 30 per cent of French PDO cheese production.

An old buronnier's memories

Jean-Louis began his life as *buronnier* when aged 15, in a *Cézallier estive*. He and his friends would remain in practically total isolation for almost five months. Life proceeded at the pace of two milkings a day and all the other tasks in between. The pasture usually was some distance from the *buron*.

An old buronnier *(artisan cheese-maker) at work in the early 20ᵗʰ century.*

L'estive, c'était quand même moins dur que le travail de la ferme, il y avait moins de nettoyage, on était plus libre. Mais quel boulot, on n'arrêtait pas ! Le petit-déjeuner était pris vers 8 heures, après cinq heures de travail : soupe au fromage, un morceau de lard, du fromage, un peu de beurre sur du pain bis la plupart du temps moisi...Pour le repas du milieu de journée, on mangeait des conserves, du saucisson qu'on prenait au crochet de la voûte du buron. Les bols et les assiettes servaient pour la semaine. On les retournait pour éviter les mouches. En 1963, notre fromage a eu le premier prix ... Il faut dire qu'il était bon. C'est la montagne qui fait le fromage, c'est bien connu, et notre montagne avait beaucoup de réglisse. [8]

The 'estive' was not as bad as the farm, the work was less hard, with less cleaning, and we were completely free. Still, it was slave's work, we never stopped! We would have breakfast around eight in the morning, after five hours of work already: cheese soup, a slab of bacon, more cheese, a pat of butter on brown bread which was mouldy most of the time ... For the noon meal, we would eat tinned food, some dry cured sausage we would take from the hook hanging from the ceiling of the *buron*. The bowls and plates would not be cleaned for a week. They were stored turned over to avoid the flies. In 1963, our cheese earned the first prize ... And good cheese it was. It is the mountain which makes the cheese, it is a known fact, and our mountain has a lot of liquorice.

Summer-grazing ('estives') in the Cézallier (Cantal). The stone huts are where the herdsmen lived; some were 'burons'. Photo: Joël Le Pelletier.

Modern Auvergne

Town and country in Clermont-Ferrand: thumbs up or down?

La ville souffre d'une image grise et surannée, mais ... dynamique économiquement, nichée dans un écrin de nature, restée à taille humaine, la capitale auvergnate offre un compromis idéal pour la vie de famille. [9]

Despite a grey and dated image, the Auvergne capital, with its healthy economy (Michelin is not the only company there), protected natural setting, and very manageable size, offers an ideal combination for family life.

But a *France-Inter* [national radio station] journalist once did some Clermont-Ferrand-bashing on air:

> *Il ne se passe rien, c'est horrible, Clermont-Ferrand ... Enfin, je ne voudrais pas insulter les Clermontois, mais c'est quand même une ville toute noire entourée de montagnes.* [10]
>
> It is completely dead, Clermont-Ferrand, it is horrible ... Actually, I don't want to hurt Clermontois feelings, but there is no denying it is a city all black and walled in by mountains.

She quickly had to make a public apology: indignant *Auvergnats* argued that Clermont-Ferrand now is the French capital of rock music, drawing in young people (many are students at its university)! Some inspired residents later fought back by filming a video using the singer Pharell Williams' 2013 hit 'Happy', as 'Happy from Clermont-Ferrand'.[11]

Ready for a change of life?

Auvergne works hard at attracting new blood: a slogan such as *'J'ai changé de vie, pourquoi pas vous?' 'L'Auvergne, ça change une vie.'*[12] ('I changed my life, why couldn't you? Auvergne just does that to you.') promotes Auvergne's quality of life. *'L'Auvergne, juste et grande'* ('Auvergne, the fair and noble one'), *'L'Auvergne, nouveau monde'* ('Auvergne, a brave new world') are other marketing slogans of the region. It even goes so far as to give financial incentives to newcomers: 'New Deal Auvergne' offers them free housing with the job during a trial period. *'L'image de la France profonde détournée en terre d'aventure pour explorateur en quête d'emploi'*[13] ('The depths of France revamped as a new frontier for job-hunting explorers') gets results: 17 000 'settlers' a year for the last few years knocked on Auvergne's door, for in this rural region, the share of industrial employment also happens to be bigger than the national average. The agro-industry sector alone is a major employer with its high-quality fresh and cured meat, the famous *charcuterie auvergnate*, cheese and dairy products, cereals and baked goods, and bottled water.

An example of Samian ware from Lezoux (Puy-de-Dôme) traded throughout the Roman Empire; this bowl was found in a Roman settlement in Britain. Photo: English Heritage.

A proud and fearless land

Harsh and austere **Auvergne** took its name from the *Arvernes*, the most powerful and prosperous Gallic tribe which led the coalition against Julius Caesar's legions. The pottery made in **Lezoux** (Puy-de-Dôme) was a household name across the Roman world. The original Auvergne — the two départements of Puy-de-Dôme and Cantal with northern Haute-Loire — was annexed by the King of France in 1271 after the constant feuding of its nobility and bishops; Velay (southern Haute-Loire), part of the former Languedoc, was added in 1790 while Bourbonnais (Allier today) was seized after the treason of Charles de Bourbon (1496-1527), the glorious cousin of King François I who defected to his arch rival, the Hapsburg Charles V. During the Hundred Years War the region, which was loyal to the French king, was repeatedly raided by English troops from the neighbouring Plantagenet possessions.

The statue of Vercingétorix in Clermont-Ferrand. Photo: Danyel Massacrier, courtesy Mairie de Clermont-Ferrand (Puy-de-Dôme).

Auvergne has produced many men and women of exceptional courage and intelligence: the Gallic commander-in-chief **Vercingétorix** (72-46 BC), who defeated the Romans at **Gergovie** (near Clermont-Ferrand) in 52 BC and became one of the two emblematic figures of French identity with Joan of Arc; two Popes, **Sylvester II** (?945-1003) and **Urbain II** (1042-1099), who ordered the First Crusade from (today's) Clermont-Ferrand; **Adhémar de Monteil** (?-1098), Bishop of Puy-en-Velay and spiritual leader of that same First Crusade; the **Marquis de La Fayette** (1757-1834) — see below, French hero of the American War of Independence; **General Desaix** (1768-1800), who fought to his death at the battle of Marengo; three Presidents of the French Republic — **Paul Doumer** (1857-1932), **Georges Pompidou** (1911-1974) and **Valéry Giscard d'Estaing** (born in 1926, who never lost his *Auvergnat* accent and did a lot to improve his region's image); the heroic *Résistants* of Mont Mouchet (Haute-Loire) in 1944, led by Colonel Gaspard **(Emile Coulaudon**, 1907-1977, a Clermont-Ferrand native); **Coco (Gabrielle) Chanel** (1883-1971), the epitome of Parisian elegance for the modern woman; great spiritual minds, such as the philosopher and scientist **Blaise Pascal** (1623-1662) — see p. 66-61 — or the mystic, scientist and explorer **Pierre Teilhard de Chardin** (1881-1955).

Germaine Tillion. Photo: Association Service Social Familial Migrants.

Germaine Tillion

Auvergnats feel very proud that **Germaine Tillion** (1907-2008), born in Allègre (Haute-Loire), was honoured with a final resting place in the Panthéon, the necropolis of great French citizens in Paris. She was an ethnologist and early *Résistante* against Nazi Germany, having created the *Musée de l'Homme Résistance* network in 1940 and survived deportation. After the war, she never stopped fighting for truth and justice: the colonized Algerians, the Algerian War and conditions in French prisons were among her causes. [Three other women were similarly commemorated, the first notably being the scientist **Marie Curie** (1867-1934) and the most recent, **Geneviève Anthonioz-de Gaulle** (1920-2002) niece of General de Gaulle and another remarkable Résistante and philanthropist like Tillion.]

Another earlier and less well-known but distinguished Auvergnate was **Angélique Le Boursier du Coudray** (1712-1789), born in Clermont-Ferrand, a *Maîtresse sage-femme* (chief mid-wife) appointed by King Louis XV to counter ignorance and barbaric practices across rural France. She wrote *L'Abrégé de l'Art des accouchements* (*The Concise Handbook on the Art of Delivering Babies*), and used a life-size doll she had designed to demonstrate safe procedures.

The Château de Chavaniac, ancestral home of the Marquis de La Fayette.
Photo: Gérard Cavaillès, Département de la Haute-Loire.

La Fayette, symbol of Franco-American friendship

Marie Joseph Paul Yves Roch Gilbert du Motier, Marquis de La Fayette was born in the family castle at **Chavaniac** [one of the many remarkable castles scattered all over Auvergne, some of them owned by the same family for centuries, and which can be admired along the *Route des Châteaux d'Auvergne*] in Haute-Loire. Strongly attached to his native Auvergne, the Marquis claimed:

J'espère être gaulois parce que très peu de Francs s'établirent dans les montagnes d'Auvergne. J'aime Vercingétorix défendant ses montagnes.[14]

I believe I am of pure Gallic ancestry since very few Franks settled in the Auvergne mountains. I love Vercingétorix defending his mountains.

A portrait of the 16-year old Marquis de La Fayette. Photo: Gérard Cavaillès, Département de la Haute-Loire.

He was aged only twenty when he volunteered to fight on the side of the American patriots:

> *Défenseur de cette liberté que j'idolâtre ... en venant comme ami offrir mes services à cette République que je trouve si intéressante.* [15]
>
> Defender and worshipper of freedom ... I came as a friend to offer my services to that Republic [of the United States], so fascinating to me.

His help for General Washington at the Battle of Yorktown (1781), backed by the troops of Comte de Rochambeau and the blockading French fleet of Admiral Comte de Grasse, made history and created a lasting bond between the United States and France. Twenty-seven towns and some ten counties in the United States carry the name of Lafayette. However, if he was called *'le héros des deux mondes'* ('the hero of both worlds'), it is because he also played an important role in France: La Fayette helped launch the Revolution of 1789, bring down Napoléon Bonaparte and establish the July monarchy after the other Revolution in 1830. Despite ultimately losing out to more pragmatic statesmen, he was a true son of the Enlightenment, relentlessly fighting against oppression and for freedom, whether for the sake of African slaves, French Protestants [he was influential in the signing of Louis XVI's *Edit de Tolérance* of 1787] or Polish political refugees.

A formal engraving of the Marquis de La Fayette. Photo: Bibliothèque Nationale de France.

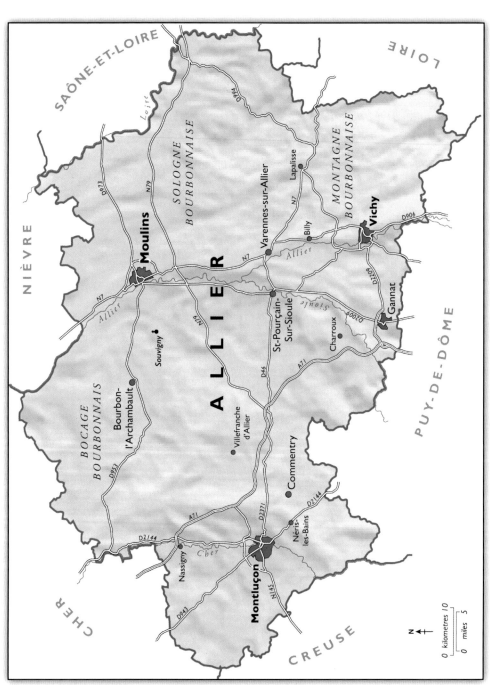

Map by Tim Aspden

The four départements of Auvergne (from north to south)

L'Allier

This Auvergnat *département* is the closest to Paris and makes the transition between 'travel book' Auvergne and *Bassin Parisien*. Its quiet and green countryside is a mosaic. Fertile **Limagne bourbonnaise** is a checkerboard of crops and includes the very ancient vineyard of **Saint-Pourçain** — it allegedly existed before the Romans — whose distinctive wines are a curiosity. The tradition of healthy bathing in thermal waters was initiated by the Romans and lives on in **Néris-les-Bains**, splendid **Bourbon-L'Archambault** and smart **Vichy**, 'the queen of French spas'.

The fortress of Bourbon-L'Archambault at the summer solstice. Photo: Daniel Blanchard, Président de l'Office du Tourisme de Bourbon-L'Archambault.

The grand interior of the thermal baths at Bourbon-l'Archambault. Photo: Joël Damasse, Routes des Villes d'Eau du Massif Central.

Historic Healing Waters in Bourbon-L'Archambault

'C'est grâce aux eaux de Bourbon-L'Archambault que je dois la vigueur de mes jambes et la verdeur de mon esprit' ('It is thanks to the thermal springs of Bourbon-L'Archambault that my legs stay nimble and my mind sharp'), so said **Charles-Maurice de Talleyrand-Périgord** (1754-1838), the great French statesman and diplomat who brilliantly managed his career through several regimes.

Les thermes de Bourbon-l'Archambault sont classés Monument National et depuis l'Antiquité, les eaux chaudes jaillies à 55° sont réputés souveraines contre les rhumatismes ... Les soins s'effectuent principalement avec des bains de vapeur et des cataplasmes de kaolin ... Les curistes au bout de trois ans consomment moins de médicaments, ont moins d'arrêts de travail et moins d'hospitalisations. [16]

Bourbon-l'Archambault spa is a National Monument and since antiquity, its hot springs bubble up at 55° ... They are credited as the ultimate remedy against rheumatism ... Treatment is with steam baths and kaolin poultices ... After three years, patients taking the waters are found to need fewer medicines, fewer sick leaves and fewer stays in hospital.

Allier, is the historic province of *Bourbonnais* and the cradle of the royal Bourbon dynasty: **Henri IV** (1553-1610) was the first of the seven Bourbon kings of France, while other branches of the family settled on thrones in Spain and Italy. The imposing twelfth-century fortress of **Billy** is a well-preserved example of past Bourbon power, along with the Cluniac abbey of **Souvigny**, the medieval city of **Moulins** — the capital of the Dukes of Bourbon — which is also endowed with the *Centre National du Costume de Scène et de Scénographie* (CNCS, National Centre of Stage Costume and Design) or historic **Montluçon**.

What is a 'lapalissade' ?

Also called *'une vérité de La Palice'*, it is a truism, a statement so obvious that it is ridiculous, such as *'He was poor because he did not have money.'* The name refers to the valiant lord of **Lapalisse** in Allier, **Jacques de Chabannes** (1470-1525), better known as Monsieur de La Palice, who was Marshal of France and was killed at the Battle of Pavia during the Wars with Italy. It is not documented that he was ever fond of this kind of verbal feat but the story goes that when he died, his soldiers praised his bravery by saying: *'Un quart d'heure avant sa mort, il faisait encore envie'* ('Fifteen minutes before his death, he still was the envy of everyone'). It would have been incorrectly recorded as: *'Un quart d'heure avant sa mort, il était encore en vie'* ('Fifteen minutes before his death, he was still alive'). A burlesque poet, **Bernard de La Monnoye** (1641-1728), composed *'La Chanson de La Palice'* ('The Song of La Palice') in that same vein: we are thus glad to know that Monsieur de La Palice met his doom on a Friday but that, had it happened on the Saturday, he would have lived longer! [17]

During the darkest days of French history, **Vichy** was chosen as the seat of *'l'Etat français'* from July 1940 to August 1944: the Vichy Regime, headed by Marshal **Philippe Pétain** (1856-1951) and an infamous *Auvergnat* 'strong man', **Pierre Laval** (1883-1945), opted for collaboration with Nazi Germany while working on the 'regeneration' of the defeated nation.

Meat production

This is the second major sector of the local economy, after water. The gentle hills and hedgerows of the **Bocage Bourbonnais** present ideal grazing conditions for the Allier-bred *Charolais* beef cattle, the first in France to obtain the *Label rouge* quality standard for first rate meat. *Tronçais* Forest is a cathedral of very tall and ancient oaks, whose wood is the choice material for the finest Bordeaux wine barrels. **Sologne bourbonnaise**, between Loire and Allier, is a corner of pristine nature, dotted with woods, streams and ponds. The south is higher, with the hills of **Combraille** (shared with Puy-de-Dôme) to the west, through which the River Sioule carves its gorges, and **Montagne bourbonnaise**, culminating at **Puy de Montoncel** (1287 m).

Jean-Luc Desnoyer with his Charolais cattle. Photo: GAEC (Groupement Agricole d'Exploitation en Commun) de la Motte-Mourgon, J-L Desnoyer - Y. Dampuré.

'*Un producteur, un savoir-faire et du goût!*' — 'A producer, savoir-faire and lots of taste!'

*A un jet de pierre de Vichy, dans l'Allier, **Jean-Luc Desnoyer**, partenaire de longue date de la démarche Origine et Qualité Carrefour, est un éleveur chevronné … Il élève son troupeau de charolaises avec beaucoup d'attention. Alimentation contrôlée — fourrage produit sur la propriété — soins quotidiens, vie au grand air la plus grande partie de l'année. 'Même si ce n'est pas scientifiquement prouvé, j'ai la conviction qu'un animal qui a eu une vie agréable donnera de la meilleure viande,' aime à rappeler l'éleveur.[18]*

Within a stone's throw from Vichy, in Allier, Jean-Luc Desnoyer, a long-time partner of the Carrefour 'Origin and Quality' premium food range, is a seasoned stock breeder … He looks after his herd of *Charolais* cattle with tender loving care. Rigorously controlled food —fodder produced on the premises — daily care, life outdoors most of the year. Even if it is not scientifically proven, I firmly believe that an animal which enjoyed a good life will develop better meat, the breeder likes to say.

As an example of the size and importance of beef production in the region, the SOCOPA slaughterhouse and meat-packing plant in **Villefranche d'Allier** processes cattle from 3800 Auvergnat farmers, yielding 1100 tons of beef per week. *Label rouge* farm-raised, free-to-roam pigs — *le porc fermier d'Auvergne* — are another speciality.

Special Auvergne pigs which roam the grassy hills, such as in the Bocage Bourbonnais area; their meat is awarded Label Rouge and IGP (PDO) distinction.
Photo: Porcs Fermiers d'Auvergne.

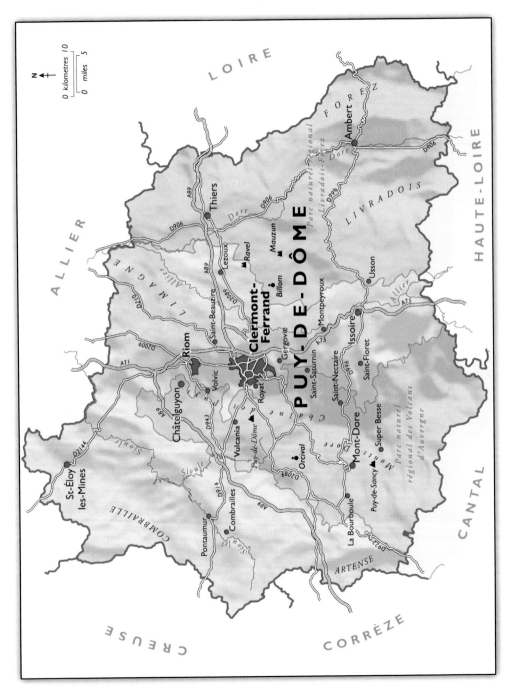

Map by Tim Aspden

Le Puy-de-Dôme

This is the most densely populated region in Auvergne, partly due to *La Limagne*, its large and fertile plain of dark volcanic soil — it is the second largest 'cereal granary' in France after *Beauce* (Centre region) — though it is not exempt from light seismic activity. The two pillars of its economy are the global companies Limagrain and Michelin. **Limagrain**, based in **Saint-Beauzire**, is the world's fourth largest company for field, vegetable and tree seeds (**Vilmorin** brand), the first in Europe for cereal products, the first in France for industrial baked goods and pastry (**Jacquet** bread and **Brossard** biscuits). It is a co-operative group managed by its Auvergnat farming members.

Clermont-Ferrand

This is the only large city in Auvergne, and is actually made up of two towns, Clairmont and Montferrand, three kilometres apart and joined in the seventeenth century. Built on a basaltic plateau, it can be seen from far away thanks to the twin black spires of its cathedral. Clermont-Ferrand's climate is notorious for its extremes in temperature (records of -29°C in winter and 40.7°C in summer) and its dryness, characteristics varying throughout the *département* because of its contrasted topography. It owes much to the **Michelin** family, who not only created a world leader in the manufacture of car tyres, maps and guides, but also took care of its employees' welfare. The saying goes: '*Quand Michelin éternue, la ville tousse*' ('When Michelin sneezes, the city coughs'). There is more than rubber in Clermont, however: a first-class rugby club, blue and yellow ASM Clermont and the *Festival international du Court-métrage* (International Short Film Festival), created by the university in 1979, which attracts some 3000 professionals every year.

The blue and yellow Michelin logo.

Bibendum, the most popular fat 'man'

The image of a pile of tyres as a grinning fat man was the brainchild of **Edouard Michelin**, who did not like to see heaps of discarded tyres unused. It was designed in 1898 after the pudgy wooden *bonshommes* (blokes) displaying menus at restaurant doors of that time. Why a grin? Because the Michelin tyre *'boit l'obstacle'* ('devours' obstacles), and because cars will take you to all kinds of interesting places where you may eat and drink (*bibendum* means 'time to drink' in Latin). Those were gentler times, but the gastronomic *Guide Michelin*, the other 'little red book', first published in 1900 and now covering restaurants in 23 countries, still is the most awaited and dreaded of its kind, removing or bestowing stars of merit as its taste dictates.

The All Auvergnat Haka of ASM Clermont

The rugby team's war cry goes along these lines:

Est-ce que vous êtes là les Auvergnats ? Whooooouw ! Qui c'est qui a dit que manger du fromage c'est mauvais pour la santé ? PAS NOUS, PAS NOOOOUS ! Qui c'est qui a dit que manger de la charcuterie c'est mauvais pour la santé ? Pas nous, PAS NOOOUS !(...).[19]

Auvergnats, are you there ? Whaoooh! Who said that eating cheese was not good for the health? Not us, NOT USSS! Who said that eating deli meats was not good for the health? Not us, NOT USSS!

Geographical features

La Limagne, with its towns of **Issoire** and **Riom**, is lower-lying territory and has plenty of sun for its *Côtes d'Auvergne* vineyards along the Allier river, but the mountains of the **Chaîne des Puys** (*Monts Dôme, Sancy Massif*) glower over Clermont-Ferrand: the northern part of the *Parc naturel régional des Volcans d'Auvergne* starts here. The unspoilt green wall of the *Limagne* Fault (*Faille de Limagne*), 3000 m at its deepest, forms both a natural barrier to urban encroachment and a showcase for the *Puys*. If the springs of **Châtel-Guyon, Le Mont-Dore, Saint-Nectaire, Royat** or **La Bourboule** spas have long-established medicinal qualities, the source at **Volvic** is familiar to millions of people who drink bottles of this notably pure mineral water, filtered through layers of volcanic rock. Deep, perfectly circular crater lakes (*Lacs Chambon, Chauvet, Pavin ...*) are set like gems amidst tree-clad slopes, while **Super Besse** is a popular ski resort in Auvergne. **Vulcania**, the European park dedicated to vulcanism, and the (very expensive) pet project of *Auvergnat* President 'VGE' (**Valéry Giscard d'Estaing**), still has to prove its profitability, so lavish were its new educational and recreational programmes.

On a more modest level, hilly **Combrailles** found another way to gain international recognition with its *Bach en Combrailles* baroque music festival honouring Johann Sebastian Bach. The **Pontaumur** church organ is a replica of the Master's in Arnstadt (Germany) brought to life by the passion of a local vet, **Jean-Marc Thiallier**, who wanted to '*faire découvrir la musique de Bach aux habitants des Combrailles et faire découvrir les Combrailles aux mélomanes avertis*' ('To introduce Bach's music to Combrailles residents and to introduce the Combrailles area to sophisticated music lovers').[20]

The Volvic *mineral water trademark is a representation of the dormant Puy de Pariou volcano near Clermont-Ferrand.*

Volvic mineral water - no worry

Née il y a une cinquantaine d'années, l'entreprise locale de bouteilles d'eau ne pensait certainement pas bouleverser à jamais le petit village de moins de 5000 habitants. La famille se contentait d'embouteiller l'eau des sources découverte dans les années trente et soixante ... La cité des tailleurs de pierre est devenue une capitale internationale de l'eau. 'Ici, on ne craint rien, il ne peut pas y avoir délocalisation. L'eau de Volvic, ce sera toujours à Volvic!' [21]

Started some fifty years ago, the local family business of bottled water never imagined it would turn its small village of 5000 inhabitants upside down for ever. It was just going about bottling the water from springs discovered in the thirties and the sixties ... The stone masons' village has become an international mineral water capital ... [Volvic lava stone has been crafted by stone masons for centuries] 'Here, there is nothing to worry about, relocation is unthinkable. Volvic water will always be in Volvic!'

Granite ranges, on the eastern side of Puy-de-Dôme, make up the ***Parc régional naturel Livradois-Forez*** (shared with Haute-Loire), where forests are densely planted with fir trees and *couzes* ('torrents') run briskly. It culminates at 1300m in the high heathlands of ***Hautes Chaumes***, home of the renowned ***Fourme d'Ambert*** cheese.

If **Ambert** and **Thiers** gave their name to time-honoured products, local castles, villages or churches are not forgotten: the medieval fortress of **Mauzun**, the 'Auvergne Giant', sits on top of a volcano, **Ravel** castle was the setting of the film '*Les Choristes*' — directed by Christophe Barratier — **Billom** holds an annual garlic fair and the austere Romanesque **Notre-Dame d'Orcival** basilica still draws pilgrims, see p. 72.

Former farm buildings (jasseries), which often were used for cheese-making, in the Hautes Chaumes area of Puy-de-Dôme. Photo: Luc Olivier, SIFAM.

Ambert: past and present fame

In the eighteenth century, **Ambert** was the capital of French paper-making; its product was praised for its whiteness and texture. The industry, however, did not survive due to the chronic lack of communications, and the Richard-de-Bas paper mill is now the ***Musée historique du Papier.***

Fourme d'Ambert, on the other hand, is alive and well. It is probably the oldest type of cheese in France, log-shaped, blue-veined and creamy.

La fourme doit son nom à la 'forme', mince moule en bois dans lequel on tasse le produit de la traite, une fois caillé, en attendant qu'une croûte se constitue à la surface. C'est cette forme qui a donné le nom de 'formage', devenu par déformation 'fromage'. [22]

'*Fourme*' gets its name from '*forme*', the thin wooden mould inside which the fresh milk, once curdled, is pressed until a crust covers its surface. It is this *forme* which gave the word '*formage*', later altered into '*fromage*'. In Auvergne, '*fourme*' is synonymous with 'cheese'.

La fabrication de la Fourme d'Ambert est tout un art. Pour permettre le développement du bleu, le fromager doit avant toute chose créer des ouvertures dans le fromage. Pour cela, il doit 'coiffer le caillé', c'est à dire favoriser le développement d'une fine peau naturelle autour du grain qui empêchera les grains de se coller complètement les uns aux autres. Ensuite, après avoir salé le fromage, il va le transpercer de part en part à l'aide d'aiguilles pour apporter l'oxygène nécessaire au développement du bleu. Il faudra enfin au moins 28 jours d'affinage pour permettre au bleu de se developer, d'abord au coeur du fromage puis vers la croûte.[23]

The making of Fourme d'Ambert is an art! The blue mould is added directly to the milk. In order to obtain the blue veins, the cheese-maker must create pockets of air inside the cheese. He has to *'coiffer le caillé'*, meaning he has to make sure that a thin skin develops around the curds to prevent them from sticking to one another. After salting the cheese [usually with dry salt as seen in the photo, but sometimes with brine], he inserts needles to let in the oxygen necessary for the growth of the blue mould. A minimum of 28 days is required for ripening, to allow the mould to spread from the centre of the cheese to its rind.

[Information courtesy of Aurélien Vorger, SIFAM (Syndicat Interprofessionnel de la Fourme d'Ambert). **www.fourme-ambert.com**]

The finished cheese in its characteristic log-shape and showing the blue mould within it. Auvergnats traditionally cut it from top to bottom; others slice across it to make it go further. Photo: Ludovic Combe, SIFAM.

(Above) Adding rennet to the milk to help curdling; the mould (Penicillium
Roqueforti) has already been added to the milk in this cheese-making process.
(Below) Salting the formed cheese before needles are inserted to create holes
through which oxygen will speed up the formation of the blue mould within. Photos:
Ludovic Combe, SIFAM.

La Maison du Pirou, an historic half-timbered medieval house in Thiers.
Photo: Service de la Communication, Mairie de Thiers.

Thiers – the cutlery capital

The panoramic, medieval town of **Thiers** is steeped in tradition: its skilled craftsmen have been forging high-precision, fine cutlery (including the famous *'Laguiole'* knife) since the fourteenth century, though the old 'metal men's' workshops are now industrial heritage sites. Twenty-first century Thiers also applies its expertise to advanced technological equipment.

The bespoke nature of
making high-class cutlery
in Thiers.
Top three photos: Gilles
Reynewaeter, Coutellerie
Thiers-Issard; lower right,
Catherine Pinchetti.

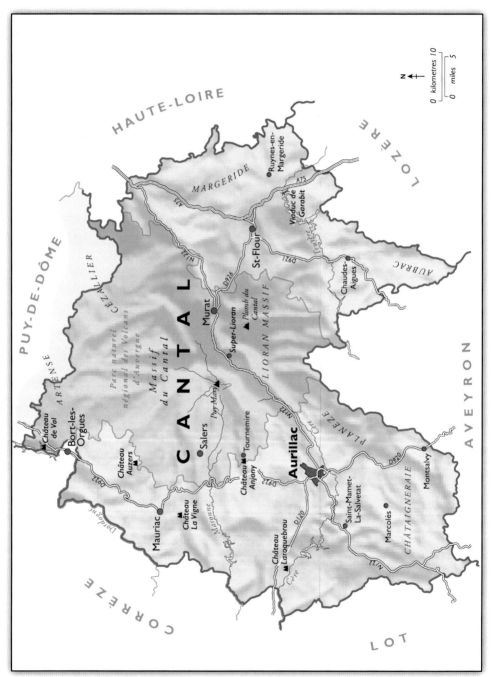

Map by Tim Aspden

Le Cantal

Geographical features

Here is one of the most beautiful and sparsely populated *départements* in France. It is surrounded by four other *Occitan* areas, Corrèze, Lot and Aveyron to the west and south, Lozère to the south-east. Named after the colossal volcano forming **Monts du Cantal** — 'cantal' is derived from a Celtic word meaning 'circle'— from which its rivers spring in star fashion, Cantal is *Haute-Auvergne*, with the highest elevations in the region. Snow is abundant, making **Super Lioran** the leading *Auvergnat* ski resort. Cantal shares *le Parc Naturel des Volcans d'Auvergne* with Puy-de-Dôme but displays perhaps the most stunning volcanic landscapes: the snow-capped *Plomb du Cantal*, abrupt **Puys** (*Puy Mary, Puy Violent...*), the grassy, windswept solitudes of basaltic plateaus, **Cézallier** which connects with Puy-de-Dôme *Monts Dore* **Planèze** west of Saint-Flour; **Artense**, with its serene highlands and lakes, is the only non-volcanic part. Beyond the Nature Park, there are the almost lunar expanses of volcanic **Aubrac**, the dense conifer forests, lakes and spectacular **Truyère** gorges in the granite wilderness of **Margeride**, the valleys of **Sumène, Cère, Goul, Lot, Célé, Alagnon, Brezons.**

The landscape of Cézallier (Cantal). Photo: Joël Le Pelletier.

It is hard to decide whether the beauty of Cantal owes more to its nature or to its built heritage. History and *Cantalienne* culture left a host of Romanesque churches and castles in sumptuous settings: **Anjony**, **Auzers**, **Laroquebrou**, **La Vigne** or **Val** in Lanobre, next to the dam of Bort-les-Orgues. Thanks to the solidity of *Auvergnat* families, villages and towns are remarkably well-preserved, with a hint of mystery, for example medieval **Marcolès**, **Montsalvy**, **Salers** or **Tournemire**. Salers, the lava-stone architectural gem, is the proud cradle of the eponymous red cattle, whose breed was improved by a local agronomist, **Ernest Tyssandier d'Escous** (1813-1889), the meaty Salers cheese and the bittersweet *Gentiane de Salers* aperitif, made from the roots of native *Gentianella lutea*.

An advertisement for the Gentiane liqueur. Note the traditional Auvergnate coif worn by the young girl.
Photo: Catherine Pinchetti;
(Below) the Gentian plant from which the liqueur is made.
Photo: Christian Lavollée.

The Viaduc-de-Garabit near Ruynes-en-Margeride (Cantal). Photo: Wikipedia.

Another man, the engineer **Gustave Eiffel** (1832-1923), architect of the Eiffel Tower in Paris, left his mark in Cantal. His daring and graceful **Garabit Viaduc**, four years in the making (1880-1884), is a lasting triumph of structural engineering, spanning the near 600m-wide *Truyère* gorges. It enabled the railway to penetrate the arduous Auvergne territory. **Chaudes-Aigues** spa boasts healing waters known before the Romans, which are the hottest in Europe — at a temperature ranging from 52 to 82°C, its fountains are steaming — and have been used to generate free heating for residents' homes since the Middle Ages! Unsurprisingly, it has a *Musée de la Géothermie*.

Cantal has an essentially rural economy. It is a champion French PDO cheese producer, supplying 70 per cent of the famed *Auvergnat* cheeses. A third of all *Cantaliens* work in this sector — *Fromageries des Monts du Cantal* in **Valuéjols** or *Fromageries Occitanes/Fromagers cantaliens* in **Saint-Mamet-la-Salvetat** are leading names — while the local dairy-farms supply all

A restored buron with its stone roof-tiles ('lauzes') clearly visible, near Murat. Photo: Christian Lavollée.

the milk for the making of the eponymous *Cantal* (39 per cent of Auvergne PDO cheeses), *Bleu d'Auvergne*, *Salers* and also several other types: untreated milk *Tomme de montagne* or *Tome fraîche*, the essential ingredients for traditional potato dishes such as *aligot* and *truffade*. The *département* is proud of its thousand-year old agro-pastoral culture: the seasonal migration of herds of cattle to *estives*, the higher summer pastures, is still massive. The precious few *burons* left — and see pp. 16-17 — those stone mountain-cabins used by herdsmen for shelter and cheesemaking, are in the care of local associations.

The pride of Cantal: the dark-red Salers cow with its characteristic lyre-shaped horns. Photo: Jean-Louis Faure, Mairie de Salers.

Aurillac

Cantal's main city, **Aurillac**, used to provide half the French population with umbrellas but the *Aurillacois* manufacturers still in business can be counted on the fingers of one hand. It has now changed its cultural fame: it teaches dance in *Choréographie La Manufacture* — housed in a former umbrella factory — created by the American choreographer **Vendetta Mathea** (born in 1953), and is turned upside down by boundless creative energy during its unique *Festival international du Théâtre de rue* (International Street Theatre Festival), which attracts over 100 000 visitors every year. **Saint-Flour**'s talent aims at the luxury market, with the fine leather works of the **Fleurus** company.

A Fine umbrella tradition: Maison Piganiol and its 'Aurillac'

The Piganiol family has been crafting high-quality umbrellas, '*les Aurillac*', since 1884 and has earned the prestigious label '*Entreprise du patrimoine vivant*' (Living Heritage Company). About 100 000 *Aurillacs*, large and made to last for generations, with a distinctive, hand-turned wooden handle, are produced every year for discriminating customers in France and abroad, notably in Japan. According to Piganiol, this is how umbrella making started in Aurillac:

Piganiol 'Aurillac' umbrellas. Photo: Catherine Pinchetti.

> *La Jordanne charriait des paillettes d'or, cet or était échangé contre du cuivre rapporté par les pèlerins venant de Saint-Jacques de Compostelle. A partir de ce cuivre étaient réalisées les pièces métalliques des parapluies. Grâce aux riches forêts cantaliennes, une industrie des mâts et des poignées en bois s'y était développée. Enfin, les paysans cantaliens qui allaient en Espagne vendre leurs chevaux ramenaient de la toile de coton avec laquelle furent confectionnées les premières couvertures. Tout était réuni pour faire d'Aurillac le berceau du parapluie français.* [24]

> Gold flakes could be panned from the Jordanne [the local river] and exchanged for the copper brought back by pilgrims from Santiago de Compostela. The copper was used for the metal parts of the umbrellas.

Thanks to the lush forests in Cantal, the masts and wood handles industry had developed. On top of that, Cantal farmers would go to Spain to sell their horses and would bring home the cotton cloth out of which the first covers were cut. In short, Aurillac had everything it needed to become the cradle of the French umbrella.

The Saints of Cantal

Saint Austremoine, the first bishop of Clermont, evangelized Auvergne in the third century. He was seconded by **Saint Mamet** — who gave his name to **Saint-Mamet-La Salvetat** — and **Saint Mary**, who is remembered for ever thanks to the *Puy Mary* volcano [no mysterious English-speaking lady involved] and whose relics are kept in a chapel overlooking the mountain. **Saint Flour**, whose original name was Florus, continued the evangelization of the region in the fourth century.

Cantal, a fisherman's paradise

Quand on survole le Cantal, en hélicoptère ou en avion, ou quand on se penche sur une carte de géographie de notre département, on est frappé par la quantité et par la densité des cours d'eau : ils s'étendent sur plus de 6 300 km, ils naissent tous au pied de nos volcans ... Pour vous rappeler une image bien scolaire, on disait que le Massif Central et le Cantal en particulier étaient le ' château d'eau de la France'. [25]

When flying over Cantal, whether by helicopter or by plane, or when looking at the geographical map of our *département*, the quantity and the density of rivers and streams is absolutely striking. Totalling more than 6,300 km, they all spring from our volcanoes foothills ... School children were always taught that the *Massif Central*, and particularly Cantal, were 'France's water capital'.

The country around Salers; the high peak in the middle distance is Puy Mary. Photo: Jean-Louis Faure, Mairie de Salers.

A lonely church in the Monts du Cantal near Le Lioran; (below) Murat (Cantal) built with dark basaltic stone. Photos: Christian Lavollée.

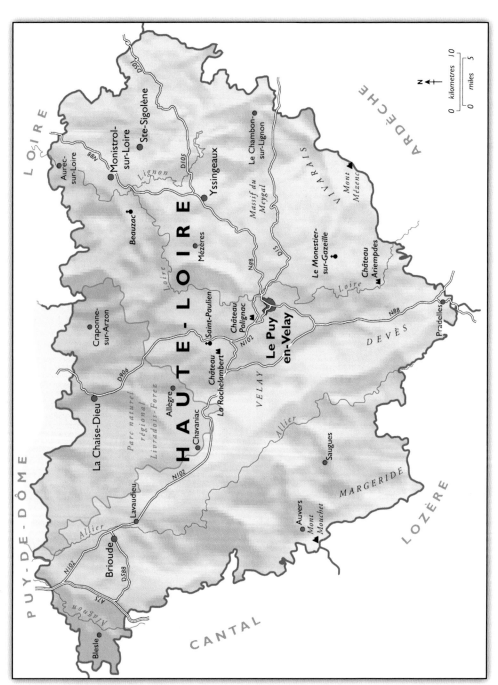

Map by Tim Aspden

La Haute-Loire

Geographical and historic features

Haute-Loire, like Cantal, is endowed with outstanding beauty, natural or historic. With an average altitude above 800 m, the *département* is one of the highest in France. It is experiencing an influx of new families, not to raise goats as in the seventies, but to enjoy a more affordable and healthier lifestyle while working along the Puy-en-Velay—Saint-Etienne or the Puy—Clermont-Ferrand axes. Haute-Loire, well linked to Lyon, Barcelona and Toulouse and favoured by the proximity of the dynamic Rhône-Alpes region, is the most attractive *Auvergnat département* to newcomers, so that previously dying villages like **Mézères** (23 km from le Puy) are being revived.

This is the territory of the 'young' Loire and 'young' Allier, its sister and main tributary, proudly called 'the last two wild rivers of (Western) Europe'. The Loire, the longest river in France, is just a bubbling stream that springs from a volcanic hillside, **Mont Gerbier de Jonc,** in Ardèche (Rhône-Alpes) and enters its gorges in the north-east of the *département*, in **Aurec-sur-Loire**. The Allier, rising in Lozère (Languedoc-Roussillon), reaches the north-western end of Haute-Loire with its own breath-taking gorges.

Haute-Loire, again like Cantal, is predominantly rural, with 90 per cent of its territory covered by forests (one third of the *département*), prairies or farmed uplands. Milk and meat — succulent **Mézenc Fin Gras**, the first *AOP* (PDO) beef in Auvergne — are the main products. Another Velay AOP, *Puy* lentils, and *Saint-Agur* creamy blue cheese gained international status, while bright green '*Verveine du Velay*' is the highly aromatic artisan spirit. Haute-Loire however also has a thriving industrial sector, which accounts for 30 per cent of its employment and is made up of small, enterprising companies. But its main success is in the plastics industry, in which it is the leading French producer of extruded polyethylene in the **Yssingeaux**

An advertisement for 'Verveine du Velay' liqueur, and Le Puy lentils, best bought in Haute-Loire.
Photos: Catherine Pinchetti.

area (**Sainte-Sigolène**). Timber products, food processing and precision metal works are also present around **Brioude**.

Tourism is Haute-Loire's greatest asset. Visitors appreciate the natural beauty and precious cultural heritage; the more active pursue white-water rafting in the river gorges, Nordic skiing in winter or hiking along the network of stunning trails. For motorcycle fans, Brioude is one of the world capitals of the Enduro World Championship: the sport started here forty years ago. **'Respirando'** (www.respirando.fr) is Haute-Loire's official label for green tourism. All kinds of outdoor activity are covered; accommodation and meals are catered for by the *Accueil paysan d'Auvergne* (Auvergne farmsteads).

The scenic Allier valley with its gorges, running south to north, gives western Haute-Loire a backbone. Called *'Pays de La Fayette'* in deference to the great man whose imposing family castle stands in Chavaniac-Lafayette – see p.22, it is dotted with beautiful medieval villages, such as **Blesle** or **Lavaudieu**, famous for its abbey. It also encompasses a part of the granitic and mysterious **Margeride**, where on **Mont Mouchet** (1497m) a Résistance Memorial rises tall and the shadow of the monstrous *Bête du Gévaudan* lingers, like the one in next-door Lozère. The beast has two museums, in **Saugues** and **Auvers**.

The St-Julien Basilica in Brioude (Haute-Loire), one of the major Romanesque churches in Auvergne.
Photo: Olivier Dessard, Ville de Brioude.

Brioude's Romanesque basilica, one of the religious treasures in Auvergne, displays the contemporary stained-glass windows created by the Korean-born (in 1940) Dominican friar and artist Kim En Joong. Another one is the majestic Saint-Robert abbey in **La Chaise-Dieu,** famous for its *Danse macabre* (Dance of Death) and its major musical and spiritual *Festival de Musique sacrée* in late summer, founded in 1966 by the pianist **George Cziffra.**

The entrance to the Château de La Rochelambert. Photo: Catherine Pinchetti.

The *La Chaise-Dieu* plateau, *Livradois-Forez* **Nature Park** (shared with Puy-de-Dôme) and *Devès* massif are the western limits of volcanic *Velay*, which numbers 300 volcanoes in the shape of spikes, basaltic organ pipes, peaks, domed *'sucs'* or crater lakes (*Lac du Bouchet)* and with an impressive variety of panoramas, particularly in the *Meygal* and *Mézenc* ranges (*Mont Mézenc*, 1753 m). Scattered among the *'Volcans en liberté'* ('Volcanoes on the loose') touristic trail and the Loire gorges are castles, from the graceful **La Rochelambert** to the eerie ruins of **Arlempdes** or the fortress of **Polignac**, medieval villages such as **Allègre, Craponne-sur-Arzon, Pradelles**, or the Auvergnat Romanesque churches of **Monestier-sur-Gazeille, Saint-Paulien** and **Beauzac**.

The rock d'Aiguilhe at Puy-en-Velay. Photo: Catherine Pinchetti.

Le Puy-en-Velay

This city, also see pp. 58-59, built of volvic black lava stone upon very steep hills, is a unique architectural achievement and a Unesco World Heritage site. It features two vertiginous basaltic rocks, the ***Rocher Corneille*** and ***Rocher d'Aiguilhe***. It is a sanctuary city, whose unusual cathedral, with its miraculous ***'Vierge noire'*** (black statue of the Virgin), was once, like Chartres, the destination of thousands of European pilgrims. It remains the original starting point of the pilgrimage to Santiago de Compostela in Spain. Le Puy-en-Velay is a living reminder of the spirituality and power of the Church in Auvergne.

Inside Le Puy-en-Velay Cathedral and the statue of St Jacques de Compostelle (Santiago de Compostela). Photos: Catherine Pinchetti.

Dentelle du Puy, the Le Puy bobbin lace, which can be traced back to the fifteenth century, is considered France's finest, and its making continues to be taught in a special school.

Examples of Le Puy lace and the bobbins used in making it. Photos: Catherine Pinchetti.

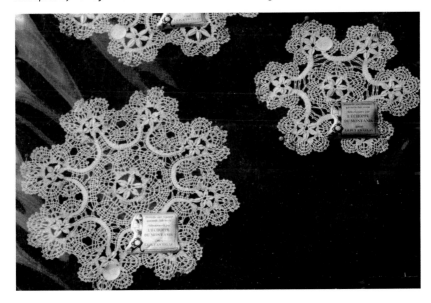

The French routes used by pilgrims to Santiago de Compostela; the Via Podiensis starts at Le Puy-en-Velay. Map: Tim Aspden.

Via Podiensis, a European and World path of faith almost twelve centuries old

> *Chaque année, ils sont près de 20 000 pèlerins, randonneurs et touristes à se lancer sur les chemins qui mènent à Saint-Jacques-de-Compostelle. Ils partent du Puy, s'aventurant sur la Via Podiensis ... En 951, quand Godescalc, l'évêque de la cité, décide de rallier les 1530 kilomètres séparant Le Puy-en-Velay de Notre-Dame de Saint-Jacques de Compostelle ... il marque la naissance du 'temps des pèlerinages' et celui du Chemin de Saint-Jacques.* [26]
>
> Every year, there are nearly 20 000, pilgrims, hikers, tourists, to take to the roads leading to Santiago de Compostela. They leave from Puy-en-Velay, their feet taking them onto the Via Podiensis ... In 951, when Puy-en-Velay's bishop, Godescalc, decided to tread the 1530 kilometres between Puy and Our Lady of Santiago de Compostela ... he launched 'the pilgrimage age' and the road to Santiago.

Gathering pilgrims from the Geneva-Lyon, or Cluny-Burgundy routes, *Via Podiensis* leads them to **Conques** (Aveyron), **Moissac** (Tarn-et-Garonne), **Roncevaux** by the Pyrenean border (Spanish Navarra) and downwards through north-western Spain (**Punta la Reina, León, Santiago**), on the route which is known as *'El Camino Francès'*.

Another path with a different purpose is the **Voie Régordane** (*Camin Régourdan* in Occitan), a 250 km scenic trail cutting through the hills of *Gévaudan* and *Cévennes* in four *départements* — Haute-Loire, Lozère, Ardèche, Gard — ending at **Saint-Gilles-du-Gard**. It was saved from oblivion by an association in the late twentieth century, and is now known as GR700 by hikers keen to get off the beaten track. The *Voie Régordane* is a *Chemin de la Tolérance*, so called because it was heavily used by soldiers (*dragonnades*) campaigning against the Protestant *Camisards* in the seventeenth century. Before that, it used to be a major trade-route when Saint-Gilles was a busy port — now well inland — and for pilgrims to the important abbey shrine there. The *route* was difficult to traverse but nevertheless was the essential link between Ile-de-France, Lower Languedoc and the Mediterranean, when the French kings did not have access to the Rhône valley, then controlled by the Germanic Holy Roman Empire till the eleventh century.

'Terre des Justes' ('Land of the Righteous among the nations'): The heroic villagers of Le Chambon-sur-Lignon

This small village on the **Vivarais-Lignon** plateau, which straddles the eastern-most part of Haute-Loire and Haute-Ardèche (Ardèche, Rhône-Alpes), has a long tradition of resistance: it was a Protestant island surrounded by Catholic *Massif Central*. During the Nazi Occupation, its residents, led by three pastors, sheltered and rescued some 1000 Jews, mostly children, and helped 5000 others to flee. The Israeli Yad Vashem Institute listed 90 of them as 'Righteous among the Nations', and awarded the whole village a distinction of honour only shared with another place in the world, **Nieuwland** in the Netherlands.

> *Du fait de leur protestantisme, ils ont toujours eu à l'esprit les persécutions religieuses dont ils ont été victimes pendant trois siècles ... Leur approche spirituelle faisait qu'ils considéraient le peuple juif comme le peuple de Dieu.* [27]
>
> Owing to their Protestant faith, they always carried in their mind the religious persecutions they had endured over three centuries ... Their spiritual approach made them consider the Jewish people as the people of God.

Le Puy-en Velay attracts a growing number of visitors every year during *les Journées du Patrimoine* (Heritage Week-End) when it re-enacts Renaissance revelry during the colourful festival of *'Le Roi de l'Oiseau'* (literally, 'King of the Bird'). In the course of one week-end, the population reverts to the sixteenth century with an elaborate representation of its sounds, rhythms, smells, gorgeous costumes, street shows and majestic parades. The climax is an archery tournament whose winner gets to be crowned *'Roi'* or *'Reine' de l'Oiseau*. Local private and public organizations and businesses contribute to the costs, alongside the *'Ponots'* (the name for Puy-en-Velay residents) and associations for the preservation of local traditions. The festival celebrates the city's heritage in the war-torn, plague and famine-stricken sixteenth century, when local patrols of city 'vigilantes' camped outside the walls to protect the population within and used to show off their might by parading in all their finery.

Paying homage to the 'Roi de l'Oiseau and his queen. Photo: Gérard Cavaillès, Service Communication, Mairie du Puy-en-Velay.

Opposite. Colourful scenes from the Renaissance festival of 'Le Roi de l'Oiseau'. Photos by: (top left) L'oiseau' itself ('le papegeai'), Théâtre de l'Alauda ; (top right) a contestant in the archery competition, Vincent Jolfre ; the fierce foot soldiers and valiant knights, families parading and ladies in their shifts treading grapes – all by Gérard Cavaillès, Service Communication, Mairie du Puy-en-Velay (Haute-Loire).

VOICES OF AUVERGNE

Bibliothèque nationale de France

Blaise Pascal (1623-1662) is Auvergne's genius. A native of Clermont-Ferrand (Puy-de-Dôme), he demonstrated an extraordinary gift for mathematics at an early age. As a scientist, he invented the first calculator, laid the foundations for infinitesimal calculus and the theory of probability and proved the existence of atmospheric pressure during his famous 1648 experiment at the bottom and top of a Puy-de-Dôme volcano (hence the pascal, unit of barometric pressure). He was a fervent Catholic and embraced Jansenism, a school devoted to strict adherence to the faith in direct conflict with the lax morals of the Jesuits. Jansenism had a profound influence on French thought in the seventeenth century but was condemned by the Catholic Church for being dangerously close to Calvin's teachings. Pascal became a theologian-philosopher, but also a sharp observer of the human comedy. He is considered to be one of the foremost French philosophers and writers — *Les Provinciales* ('The Provincial Letters') and *Les Pensées* ('Thoughts'). Many of his sayings have become words of wisdom frequently quoted in educated French conversations.

'Pourquoi me tuez-vous? - Eh quoi! Ne demeurez-vous pas de l'autre côté de l'eau? Mon ami, si vous demeuriez de ce côté, je serais un assassin et cela serait injuste de vous tuer de la sorte ; mais puisque vous demeurez de l'autre côté, je suis un brave et cela est juste.'

'Why are you killing me? What? Don't you dwell on the other side of the water? My friend, if you dwelled on this side, I would be a murderer and it would be unfair to kill you in that way, but since you live on the other side, I am a hero and it is fair.'

'Mien, tien. «Ce chien est à moi,» disaient ces pauvres enfants. «C'est là ma place au soleil.» Voilà le commencement et l'image de l'usurpation de toute la terre.'

Mine, yours. 'This dog is mine,' those poor children would say. 'This is my place under the sun.' Here is the beginning and the image of usurpation all over the earth.

L'homme n'est qu'un roseau, le plus faible de la nature; mais c'est un roseau pensant. Une vapeur, une goutte d'eau suffit pour le tuer. Mais quand l'univers l'écraserait, l'homme serait encore plus noble que ce qui le tue, parce qu'il sait qu'il meurt, et l'avantage que l'univers a sur lui ; l'univers n'en sait rien.

Man is but a reed, the weakest in nature, but he is a thinking reed. A vapour, a drop of water are enough to kill him. Yet, even if the universe would crush him, Man would still be more noble than that which is killing him, because he knows he is dying, and he knows the advantage that the universe has over him; the universe knows nothing of it.

[English translation by Catherine Pinchetti.]

The statue of Blaise Pascal at Clermont-Ferrand.
Photo: Fernand Pujos ; Bibliothèque nationale de France.

Bibliothèque nationale de France

Jules Vallès (1832-1885) was a native of Puy-en Velay (Haute-Loire). For a long time, he was excluded from the pantheon of major French writers (i.e., those featured in the French literature school curriculum). The problem was that Jules Vallès was a rebel, tirelessly waving the red flag of revolt: against the family (after an unhappy childhood), against education ('school breeds 'parrots''), against all forms of dictatorship (one solution, Revolution). He was another *Auvergnat* who made it to Paris, where he became one of the most flamboyant and reckless political journalists of his time. No censorship, no jail could ever quench his fury. He experienced the Socialist dream of his life with the Commune episode in 1871 and feverishly published his famous newspaper, *Le Cri du peuple.* He was sentenced to death after the tragic ending of the Commune, and spent nine years of exile in London, writing his masterpiece, the trilogy of *Jacques Vingtras* — *L'Enfant* ('The Child'), *Le Bachelier* ('The Graduate'), and *L'Insurgé* ('The Rebel'). It is a tale of sorrow and struggle, lightened by a pervasive sense of humour. On the day of Vallès' funeral, back in Paris after the general amnesty, thousands of factory workers, former *communards* and left-wing journalists escorted his body to the Père-Lachaise cemetery ...

La distribution des prix est dans trois jours ... Comment Mme Vingtras habillera-t-elle son fruit, son enfant, son Jacques? Il faut qu'il brille, qu'on le remarque. On est pauvre, mais on a du goût. Elle s'égratigne enfin à une étoffe criante, qui a des reflets de tigre au soleil. 'Jacques, je vais te faire une redingote avec ça!' La redingote est prête ... Non, Jacques, elle n'est pas prête. Ta mère t'aime, et veut te le prouver ... Et ne la vois-tu pas qui joue, à la fois orgueilleuse et modeste, avec des noyaux verts? ... Ces noyaux sont des boutons vert vif, vert gai, en forme d'olives, qu'on va ... coudre tout le long 'à la polonaise'. 'A la polonaise', Jacques! Ah! Quand plus tard il fut dur pour les Polonais, quoi d'étonnant? Le nom de cette nation, voyez-vous, resta chez lui cousu à un souvenir terrible ... la redingote de la distribution des prix, la redingote à noyaux, aux boutons ovales comme des olives et verts comme des cornichons ...

Prize-giving is in three days ... How will Mme Vingtras [the author's mother] dress the fruit of her womb, her child, her Jacques? He must shine, be noticed. They may be poor but they have taste ... Her hand ruffles a gaudy fabric, which bears a striking resemblance to a sun-bathed tiger ... 'Jacques, I am going to make you a smart frock coat with that!' ... The frock coat is now ready. Wrong, Jacques, it is not ready. Your mother loves you, and she will prove it ... Don't you see her, proud and modest at the same time, fiddling with green things which look like fruit stones? ... Those stones are bright green, cheerful green buttons, olive-shaped, and they are going to be sewn along the whole length, 'Polish-style'. 'Polish-style', mind you, Jacques! Ha! When later on he turned against the Poles, it was hardly surprising! The very name of that nation, you see, recalled a ghastly memory ... the prize-giving frock coat, the one with fruit-stones, oval buttons like olives, as green as gherkins ...

[English translation by Catherine Pinchetti.]

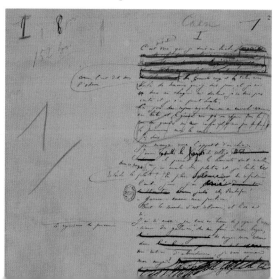

Part of the first page of the manuscript of Jules Vallès' L'Insurgé. Source: Bibliothèque nationale de France.

babelio

Antoine Sylvère (1888-1963) whose only known picture is above, was born in Ambert (Puy-de-Dôme) to a family of very poor tenant farmers. His life is like a novel: a harsh, cheerless childhood, brutal factory work at 13, the Foreign Legion at 17 to escape a sentence of twenty years of forced labour for theft, and then, the social climb: armed with a hard-earned engineering degree, he resuscitated several sugar factories in northern France after the First World War. He was discriminated against by a bourgeoisie to which he did not belong, gravitated to Paris like so many of his Auvergnat contemporaries and started to write. He denounced social injustice and became actively involved in the *Résistance* movement during the Nazi occupation. His autobiographical novel, *Toinou, le cri d'un enfant auvergnat*, is one of those rare books bearing witness to the French peasantry's life before the two World Wars. 'Toinou' did not even know how to speak French before he started school, for *Auvergnats* used an Occitan dialect, now revived in clubs or associations.

[The extracts on the opposite page are © Editions PLON, Département d'Edi8, Paris, reprinted with kind permission of the Publisher; English translation by Catherine Pinchetti.]

[Toinou remembers his paternal grandfather, Old Toinou]

Je n'ai pas d'autre exemple d'un homme ayant pu, comme le vieux Toinou, vivre sur un bien si pauvre. Ses chèvres lui donnaient un peu de lait. Il en fabriquait des fromages, qu'il vendait au marché. C'était là son seul moyen de faire de l'argent liquide ... Cela lui permettait d'acquérir avec parcimonie les produits indispensables qu'il ne tirait pas de son propre fonds. Ses chaussures, simples sabots de frêne, étaient si bien entretenues, si savamment cloutées, qu'il parvenait à les faire durer des années ...

I have never met another man who could have survived on such meagre means. His goats gave him some milk. He would make cheese with it, to be sold at the market. That constituted his only source of cash ... The money enabled him to purchase, parsimoniously, the bare necessities he could not generate on his own. His shoes, rustic ash wood clogs, were so well taken care of, so expertly nailed, that he would manage to make them last for years ...

[His maternal grandfather, *Le Grand,* is the only one who gave him love in his childhood and was his first teacher.]

La nuit tombée, nous regardions les étoiles.

'Elles ont toutes des noms. Mais ceux qui les connaissent les gardent pour eux comme un secret. Toi, faudra que tu ailles dans les villes où on peut apprendre tout ça. Y aura pas de terre pour toi. Y a rien qui te retiendra.'

Et il terminait par ce conseil :

'Ce qu'on voudra pas te dire, faudra pas avoir peur de le voler. Si t'as bien dans la tête l'idée d'apprendre, le tonnerre de Dieu pourra pas t'en empêcher ...'

After nightfall, we would gaze at the stars.

'They all have names. But those who know them keep it to themselves like a secret. You, you'll have to go to the city where you will learn all that. There will be no land for you. Nothing to hold you back.'

And he would end with this advice:

'Whatever won't be disclosed to you, don't be afraid to take it. If you are determined in your head to learn, not even God's thunder will stand in your way ...'

Bibliothèque nationale de France

Jules Romains (1885-1972) is another Parisian *Auvergnat*. He was born in Saint-Julien-Chapteuil in Haute-Loire, but was actually named Louis Henri Farigoule, the son of a *Velay* family who later moved to Paris. Louis, known as Jules, grew up in Montmartre, read philosophy at the prestigious Ecole Normale Supérieure and ended up a member of the Académie française. He was the founder of the Unanimist literary movement and a firm believer in the 'collective soul', the solidarity of the group transcending individual existence. His humanistic ideal permeates his gigantic work in 27 volumes, *Les Hommes de bonne volonté* ('Men of Goodwill'), which painted a picture of political and social life in 1908-1933 Europe. But it was his plays that have stood the test of time far better: his satirical play, *Knock ou le Triomphe de la médecine* (1923), first staged with the famous actor Louis Jouvet as Dr Knock, is his masterpiece. It later became a film with the same name, and remains one of the most popular French comedies of all time with audiences all over the world, and a model of the French language at its wittiest.

[The action in *Knock* is set in the imaginary small mountain village of Saint-Maurice, which bears a resemblance to the author's birthplace: bills are paid at Michaelmas; market day is the main local event; the town crier, the *instituteur* (primary school teacher), the chemist and the innkeeper are precious allies; and the sturdy farmers are as tight with their money as they are gullible. They fall prey to a greedy young doctor from the city who starts off giving free consultations and eventually converts them all into being hypochondriacs.]

Knock: 'Ah! Voici les consultants. Une douzaine, déjà ? Prévenez les nouveaux arrivants qu'après onze heures et demie je ne puis plus recevoir personne, au moins en consultation gratuite. C'est vous qui êtes la première, madame ? (Il fait entrer la dame en noir et referme la porte.) (...)

La dame: J'habite la grande ferme qui est sur la route de Luchère.

Knock: Elle vous appartient ?

La dame: Oui, à mon mari et à moi.

Knock: Si vous l'exploitez vous-même, vous devez avoir beaucoup de travail.

La dame: Pensez ! monsieur, dix-huit vaches, deux bœufs, deux taureaux, la jument et le poulain, six chèvres, une bonne douzaine de cochons, sans compter la basse-cour. (...)

Knock: Je vous plains. Il ne doit guère vous rester de temps pour vous soigner.

La dame: Oh! non.

Knock: Et pourtant vous souffrez.

La dame: Ce n'est pas le mot. J'ai plutôt de la fatigue.

Knock: Oui, vous appelez cela de la fatigue. (...)

[Knock carries on an examination of the lady and concludes that she is suffering from the consequences of a fall from a ladder a long time ago.]

Knock: Vous aviez déjà consulté le docteur Parpalaid ? (His predecessor, who had no business sense)

La dame: Non, jamais.

Knock: Pourquoi ?

La dame: Il ne donnait pas de consultations gratuites. (Un silence)

Knock (il la fait asseoir) : Vous vous rendez-compte de votre état ?

La dame: Non.

Knock (il s'assied en face d'elle) : Tant mieux. Vous avez envie de guérir ou vous n'avez pas envie ?

La dame: J'ai envie.

Knock: J'aime mieux vous prévenir tout de suite que ce sera très long et très coûteux. (...)

La dame: Et combien que ça me coûterait ? (...)

Knock: Eh bien! ça vous coûtera à peu près deux cochons et deux veaux.

La dame : Ah! là là! C'est une désolation, Jésus Marie ! (...) Oh! là là! J'ai eu bien du malheur de tomber de cette échelle ! (...) Et en faisant ça plus...grossièrement, vous ne pourriez pas me guérir à moins cher ?

© Editions Gallimard, Paris

Knock: Here come the patients. A dozen, already? Let the new ones know that past eleven thirty I cannot see anyone, at least for a free consultation? So, you are the first, Madam? (He brings in the lady in black and closes the door.) (...)

The lady: I live in the big farm on the road to Luchère.

Knock: You own it?

Lady: Yes, me and my husband.

Knock: If you manage it yourself, you must have a lot of work.

Lady: You could not be more right, sir! Eighteen cows, two oxen, two bulls, the mare and the colt, six goats, a good dozen of pigs, not to mention the farmyard. (...)

Knock: I pity you. You must not find time to take care of yourself.

Lady: Certainly not!

Knock: And yet, you are in pain.

Lady: I would not put it this way. I feel tired, that's more like it.

Knock: Yes, you call that 'tiredness' ... Did you see Dr Parpalaid [his predecessor] before ?

Lady: No, never.

Knock: Why ?

Lady: He would not give free consultations. [Silence]

Knock [he makes her sit down]: Are you aware of your condition ?

Lady: No.

Knock [he sits across from her]: That's a blessing. Would you like to be healthy or not?

Lady: I would.

Knock: I have to be frank with you: it will be very long and very costly. (...)

Lady: And just how much would it cost me? (...)

Knock: Well, it would cost you approximately two pigs and two calves.

Lady: Help me God! It is a disaster, Jesus, Mary mother of God! ... Lord have pity! I really had bad luck to fall from that ladder! ... And if you did the job ... not so thoroughly, could you not heal me for less?

[English translation by Catherine Pinchetti.]

babelio

Jean Anglade was born in 1915 in Thiers (Puy-de-Dôme). He was the son of a mason and a housemaid and originally a joiner. He taught himself all the way to qualifying as a teacher. His first novel, written in 1952, *Le Chien du Seigneur* (*The Lord's Dog*) was the start of a hugely prolific literary career: over 90 titles, ranging from biographies (*Pascal l'insoumis* — *Pascal the Rebel)* and history books (*Histoire de l'Auvergne*, 1974; *Une vie en rouge et bleu: la Guerre vue par le dernier des Poilus* — Life in Red and Blue: the Great War seen by the last of the French *Poilus*, 2010) to essays, scenarios and comic books. Hailed as '*le Pagnol auvergnat*' ('Auvergne's Marcel Pagnol'), he lovingly set his novels in his native region: for instance, his acclaimed trilogy, *Les Ventres Jaunes* (*The Yellow Bellies*), *La Bonne Rosée* (*The Good Dew*) and *Les Permissions de Mai* (*Leaves of Absence in May*), narrates the life of Thiers knife-makers from the late nineteenth century to the middle of the twentieth , while *Le Roi des fougères* (*King of the Ferns*, 1996) is set in Clermont-Ferrand. Jean Anglade was awarded the *Prix du Roman populiste* for *L'Immeuble Taub*, 1957, and *Prix des Libraires* for *La Foi et la Montagne*, 1962.

Un Cœur Etranger (Someone Else's Heart, 2008), once again set in Clermont-Ferrand, is the moving story of the crossing of two lives: Auvergnat Armand Chaumette, a doctor and cardiac patient in Orcival, and Jules Stapinski, the deceased son of a Nord-Pas-de-Calais coal miner of Polish origin. The former receives the latter's heart and cannot rest until he finds his donor's identity in order to express his gratitude.

[A description of Clermont-Ferrand]

'*Pour l'apprécier dans son ensemble, il fallait s'approcher de la ville sans courir. En venant de Thiers, le soir, quand le soleil déjà mort emplissait le ciel du sang de son agonie. Les puys alignés formaient un divan de velours violet sur lequel, bien à l'aise, l'ancienne Augustonemetum allongeait ses membres fatigués. Sur le tout, la cathédrale dressait ses deux flèches pareilles au V de la victoire. (...) Ou même attendre la nuit complète. Alors ses lignes disparaissaient, remplacées par des lumières. (...) Leur débordement ruisselait dans la plaine ; il embrasait les premières pentes des montagnes. (...) C'était superbe et redoutable. Car de même que Paris pompe la France, Clermont pompe la substance humaine de l'Auvergne.*'

'To take it all in, you had to gradually get closer to the city, without rushing. Coming from Thiers, in the evening, when the sun had set, filling the sky with the blood it had shed in its last throes. The row of *puys* formed a purple velvet sofa, cradling the tired limbs of ancient *Augustonemetum* (Roman name of Clermont). Towering over everything, the two spires of the cathedral would carve the 'V' of victory in the sky. Or better, you could wait until nigh had fallen. Then the outline of the city would disappear and be replaced by lights. (...) They spilled into the plain; they set on fire the first slopes of the mountains. (...) It was splendid and terrible. For, as France is sucked in by Paris, Auvergne's human substance is sucked in by Clermont.'

[Extracts from *Un Cœur étranger* de Jean Anglade. © Presses de la Cité, un département de Place des Editeurs, Paris, 2008. English translations by Catherine Pinchetti.]

[on Orcival Basilica]

'*Un des chefs-d'œuvre de l'art roman auvergnat, avec ses grandes toitures de pierre, elle semble la sœur aînée des maisons environnantes. (…) A l'intérieur, une Vierge assise sur son trône avec une royale raideur, tient sur ses genoux son fils aux proportions d'adulte.(…) Elle est le type de ces Vierges auvergnates dites de majesté, dont le genre fut créé au IXème siècle par le moine Aleaume, orfèvre et sculpteur, architecte aussi de la cathédrale de Clermont.(…) Chaque année, le grand pèlerinage de l'Ascension lui amène des milliers de fidèles et des cierges. (…) A la façade de la basilique sont suspendus des carcans, des chaînes, des boulets. Hommage d'anciens captifs libérés. La Vierge d'Orcival s'appelle aussi Notre-Dame de la Délivrance ou Notre-Dame des Fers. Des milliers de déportés sont venus la remercier après 1945 pour avoir échappé à l'extermination. On pique-nique dans les prairies au milieu des vaches rouges. On danse la bourrée. Une immense exaltation emplit ce val.*'

'One of the masterpieces of *Auvergnat* Romanesque art, it has big stone roofs which make it look like the older sister of the houses around it. (…) Inside, a queenly Virgin sits erect, holding on her lap her child son with adult proportions. (…) She is of the *Auvergnat* 'Majesty' Virgin type, created in the ninth century by the monk Aleaume, a goldsmith, sculptor and also the architect of Clermont Cathedral. (…) Every year, the major Ascension pilgrimage brings thousands of faithful with their church candles. (…) Iron collars, shackle balls and chains hang from the frontage of the basilica. Tokens of gratitude from freed prisoners in the past. The Orcival Virgin is known as Our Lady of Deliverance or Our Lady of the Irons. After 1945, thousands of deportees made the trip to thank her for having been spared extermination. People have picnics in the meadows, next to the red cows. They dance '*bourrée*'. The whole vale is brimming with exaltation.'

Orcival Basilica. Photo: www.musicales-orcival.eu

Bibliographic references

1 *Destination Grand Sud / Viaduc Magazine*, n° 6, déc./jan./fév. 2006.

2 *Respirando, Activités de pleine nature en Haute-Loire (Mission départementale du développement touristique de la Haute-Loire)*. www.respirando.fr

3 DARGENT, Nathalie. *Ces Provinciaux qui ont fait Paris.* Paris : Sélection du Reader's Digest, 2008.

4 www.lexpress.fr, (François Dufay, interview de Jean Anglade), 31/07/2008.

5 www.regardsetviedauvergne.fr

6 *La Montagne*, éd. du Cantal, 16/12/2010.

7 *Saveurs Magazine*, (on Cantal cheese), *août* 1999.

8 www.burons-du-cantal.fr, (recueilli par Jacques Hamon).

9 *L'Express*, 'Où vit-on le mieux en France ?', 10/05/2004.

10 www.cyberbougnat.net, 06/02/2012.

11 www.youtube.fr ('Happy from Clermont-Ferrand' song, Guillaume Prémilhat, La Petite Boîte auvergnate, 2013. Other version by Arnaud Mazard and Mathieu Mougel.)

12 www.auvergnelife.tv.

13 www.lefigaro.fr (Sébastien Thévenet), 12/11/2012.

14 TAILLEMITTE, Etienne. *La Fayette.* Paris : Fayard, 1989. Quotation from the original *'Mémoires, correspondance et manuscrits du général de La Fayette'*, listed in his bibliography.

15 www.videos.tf1.fr, , 16/04/2012.

16 www.historia.fr, (on Monsieur de La Palice), 3 *janvier 2013*.

17 Carrefour Supermarkets *Publi-communiqué*, March 2014 (*Origine et Qualité, Jean-Luc Desnoyer, éleveur à Bost et ses charolaises*).

18 www.cyberbougnat.net, 30 avril 2013.

19 *Massif Central Magazine*, (on Bach in Combrailles Festival), *juillet-août 2004*. Le Puy : Velay Presse, 2004.

20   *Destination Grand Sud/Viaduc Magazine* n°6 *(op.cit.)*.

21   HENNEQUIN Bernard, dir. *Richesses des terroirs de France*. Paris : Bordas/France Loisirs, 1994.

22   Information on the making of Fourme d'Ambert, as given by Aurélien VORGER, SIFAM (Syndicat Interprofessionnel de la Fourme d'Ambert.

23   Maison Piganiol, Aurillac (Cantal).

24   www.cantalpassion.com, 31/03/2012.

25   *Destination Grand Sud/Viaduc Magazine* n°6 *(op.cit.)*.

26   www.lefigaro.fr, (Joanna Zilberstein), 02/06/2003. The quotation is from Patrick CABANEL, co-author of the book: '*La Montagne, refuge, accueil et sauvetage des Juifs du Chambon*'. Paris: Albin-Michel, 2013.

Voices of Auvergne

PASCAL, Blaise. *Pensées*. Paris : Classiques Hachette, 1967.

VALLÈS, Jules. *L'Enfant*. Paris : Gallimard, Folio Classique, 2000.

SYLVÈRE, Antoine. *Toinou, le cri d'un enfant auvergnat*. Paris : Plon/France Loisirs, 1980.

ROMAINS, Jules. *Knock ou le Triomphe de la médecine* (édition d'Annie Angremy). Paris : Gallimard, coll. Folio Théâtre, 1993.

ANGLADE, Jean. *Un cœur étranger*. Paris : Presses de la Cité, 2008.

Not to be missed:

Villes et Pays d'Art et d'Histoire: Moulins, Montluçon (Allier), Riom, Clermont-Ferrand, Forez, Dauphiné d'Auvergne (Puy-de-Dôme), Haut-Allier, Le Puy-en-Velay (Haute-Loire).

Plus beaux Détours de France: Lapalisse, Néris-les-Bains (Allier), Ambert, Issoire (Puy-de-Dôme), Saint-Flour (Cantal), Le Puy-en-Velay (Haute-Loire).

Plus Beaux Villages de France: Charroux (Allier), Montpeyroux, Saint-Floret, Saint-Saturnin, Usson (Puy-de-Dôme), Salers, Tournemire (Cantal), Arlempdes, Blesle, Lavaudieu, Pradelles (Haute-Loire).

Parc naturel régional des Volcans d'Auvergne,
Parc naturel régional Livradois-Forez.

UNESCO World Heritage Site: Le Puy (Cathedral and Hôtel-Dieu, as parts of Routes to Santiago de Compostela in France).

Regional websites
www.cr-auvergne/fr
www.auvergne-tourisme.info
www.parcdesvolcans.fr
www.chainedespuys-failledelimagne.com
www.planete-auvergne.com
www.auvergne-centrefrance.com
www.art-roman.net/auvergne/auvergne.htm
www.route-chateaux-auvergne.org
www.fromages-aop-auvergne.com
www.ot-bourbon.com
www.ville-thiers.fr
www.thiers-tourisme.fr
www.burons-du-cantal.fr
www.salers.fr
www.chateau-lafayette.com
www.ville-brioude.fr
www.lepuyenvelay.fr
www.ot-lepuyenvelay.fr

Regional newspapers
La Montagne, www.lamontagne.fr

Universities
Clermont-Ferrand:
Université Blaise Pascal: univ-bpclermont.fr
Université de Clermont-Ferrand: www.u-clermont1.fr
[Note: the two will merge in 2017 and become Université Clermont-Auvergne.]

Regional acknowledgements

Our warmest thanks go to the following contributors, who kindly shared with us photographs illustrating their region:

ALLIER

BOURBON-L'ARCHAMBAULT : Office de Tourisme de Bourbon-L'Archambault, M. Daniel BLANCHARD, Président.

Route des Villes d'Eaux du Massif Central, Mme Léa LEMOINE, chargée de mission Patrimoine.

MAGNET : GAEC de la Motte-Mourgon, MM. Jean-Luc DESNOYER & Y. DAMPURÉ.

MONTLUÇON : APVC Porcs Fermiers d'Auvergne, Mme Hélène DAVIET, Communication.

PUY-de-DÔME

AMBERT : SIFAM (Syndicat Interprofessionnel de la Fourme d'Ambert), MM. Aurélien Vorger, animateur, Nicolas DUMONT, Luc OLIVIER et Ludovic COMBE, Photographes.

AUBIÈRE: Association des Fromages AOP d'Auvergne, Mme Véronique HUCAULT.

CLERMONT-FERRAND: Mairie, Mme Hélène RICHARD, Photothèque, Service de la Communication, M. Danyel MASSACRIER, photographe de la Ville de Clermont-Ferrand.

THIERS: Mairie, Mme Sarah SANCHEZ, Service de la Communication.

Coutellerie Thiers-Issard, M. Gilles REYNEWAETER, Président.

CANTAL

SALERS: Mairie, M. Jean-Louis FAURE, Maire de Salers.

HAUTE-LOIRE

BRIOUDE: Mairie, M. Olivier DESSARD, Service de la Communication.

LE PUY-en-VELAY: Conseil général de la Haute-Loire, Mme Karine ROCHE, Service Communication et Relations Presse.

Mairie, M. Marc CIVEYRAC, Service Communication.

Association Théâtre de l'Alauda (Roi de l'Oiseau), Mme Véronique DUMOULIN.

We are very grateful to **ASSFAM (Association Service Social Familial Migrants, www.assfam.org)** for the photo of Germaine Tillion.

We also wish to thank **RANDO POUR TOUS** Hiking Club (Bois-le-Roi, Seine-et-Marne), M. Christian LAVOLLÉE, Président and the members who contributed beautiful photos of the Lioran Massif (Cantal) and Puy de Sancy (Puy-de-Dôme).

Appendix 1

Map of the Cathar (Occitan-speaking) territory. Map by Tim Aspden, source Pyrénées Magazine.

Appendix 2

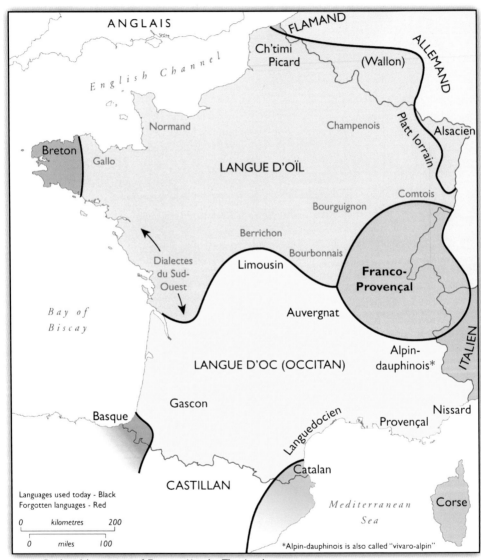

Regional languages of France. Map by Tim Aspden.

Index

Many burons and jasseries have been adapted to new uses.
Photo: André Guillot.